The Sonshine's Jewels

Diane B Jordan

The Sonshine's Jewels

Xulon Press
2301 Lucien Way #415
Maitland, FL 32751
407.339.4217
www.xulonpress.com

© 2019 by Diane B Jordan

All rights reserved solely by the author. The author guarantees all contents are original and do not infringe upon the legal rights of any other person or work. No part of this book may be reproduced in any form without the permission of the author. The views expressed in this book are not necessarily those of the publisher.

Unless otherwise indicated, Scripture quotations taken from the King James Version (KJV)–*public domain.*

Printed in the United States of America.

ISBN-13: 978-1-5456-7931-9

This book is dedicated to Jesus Christ, my LORD, Savior and King.
I give this book back to You because You gave it to me.

for
Cody Kaseem Kyaira Ky'mani Chad Caleb
I Love You
Fulfill Your Purpose
Be Jewels That Shine
For The Son

To
Pastor J Dykeman Brown<>Pastor Sandra Brown
Thank you for provoking to purpose to fulfill connections intended
To God Be The Glory

For My Sons & Daughters, My Entire Family
Thank You, I Love You

Hi.

We are...

The Sonshine's Jewels.

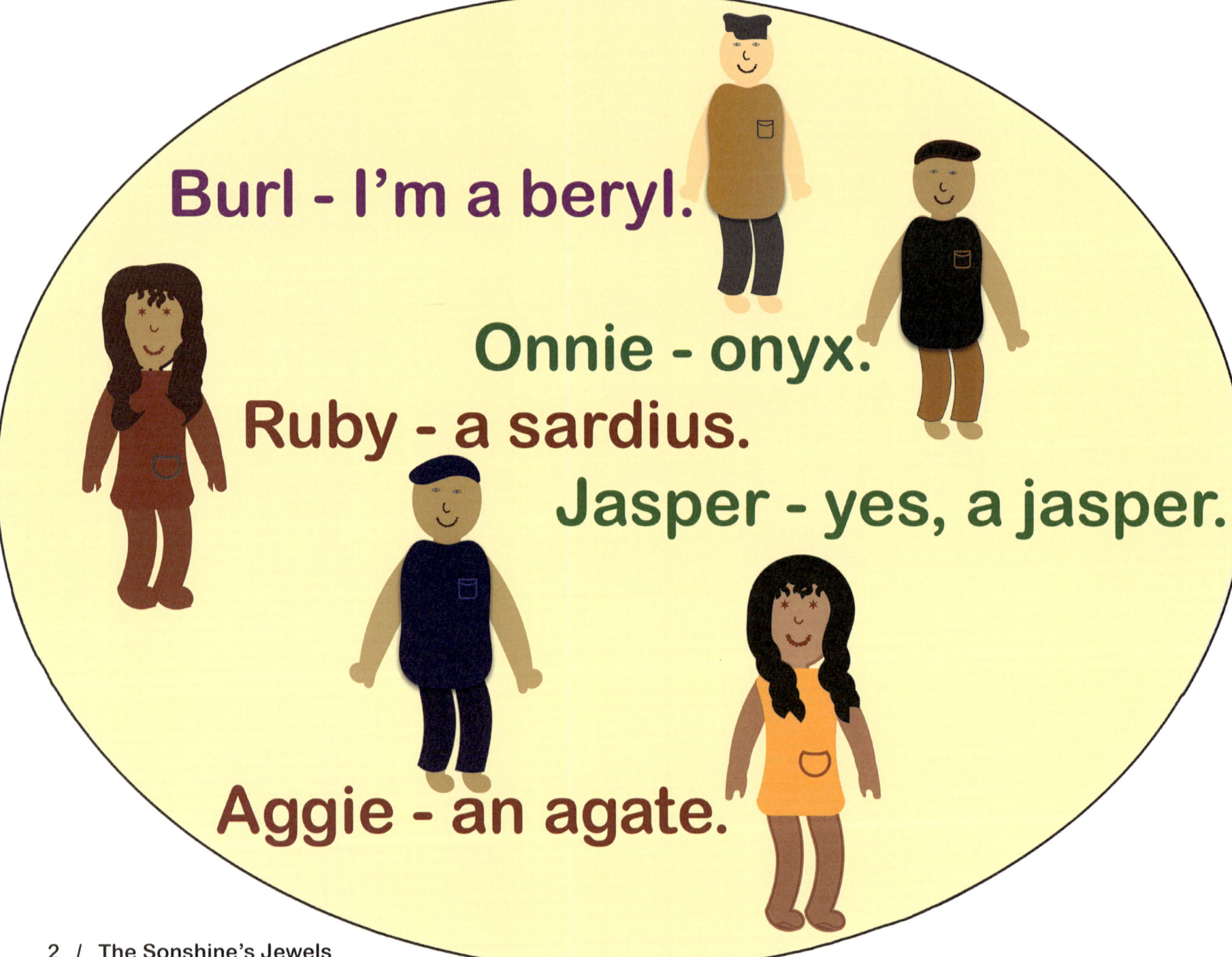

We live in a very
special place.

You can find us in The Bible.

Our address is:
 New Jerusalem Revelations Chapter 21 verses 19 and 20

(Revelations 21:19,20)

We are also in the Old Testament

Exodus 28:15-21

[17-20]…first row…a sardius…third row…an agate…
fourth row a beryl, and an onyx, and a jasper:…

The LORD has something to share with you, to tell you.

GET READY!!!

Come...,

hear.

It is The Fear of The LORD!

WOW!

What does <u>that</u> mean?

It means you will be wise...
Proverbs 15:33

have a GREAT love for God so that you want to listen and obey when He speaks... Deuteronomy 4:10

With my ears and my heart.

The FEAR of the LORD will help you go away from evil…
Proverbs 3:7

When we FEAR The LORD...

we walk in His ways... Deuteronomy 8:6

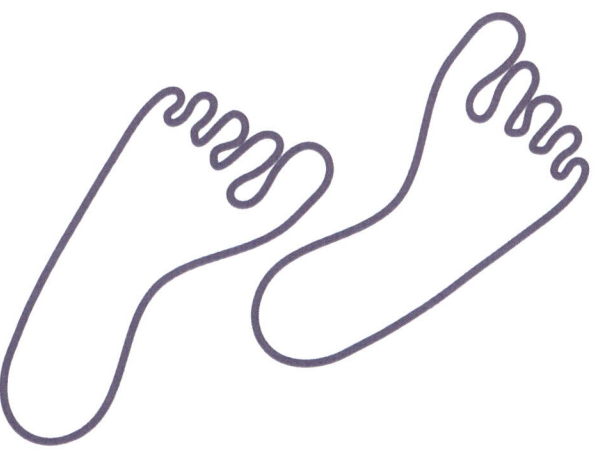

serve Him with all our heart… ♡

Deuteronomy 10:12, 20

ALL my heart!
Yeah!

Give God my time... give Him the best of the first of everything we do or receive... Deuteronomy 14:23 (IT IS CALLED TITHE) (long i sound-silent e) t i t h ...my money, and be happy doing it!

have no other gods to take His place…
Joshua 24:14

 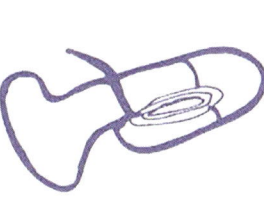 

There's more…

The Fear of The LORD is a fountain of life
Proverbs 14:27

Awesome…

(it keeps you from traps/things that draw you away from God)

Aggie adds, like ABCs... 1-2-3, love...

The Fear of The LORD is the beginning of knowledge-how we start to know things

Proverbs 1:7

The Fear of The LORD prolongeth days-helps you live a long time

Proverbs 10:27

The Fear of The LORD is strong confidence-it helps you know you can do what He says to do

I can do all things through Christ...

Proverbs 14:26

When we Fear the LORD, it keeps us living and feeling very good about loving Him…

…living long and loving The LORD…

...and then it will keep evil away-we will not want to do anything bad.

Proverbs 19:23

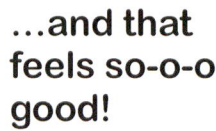
...and that feels so-o-o good!

Be happy!
The Fear of The LORD
makes you so!

Proverbs 28:14

Almost Burl…

Just a little more:

Hey Ruby, are we done?

"Onnie, that's great!"

"Yeah, God is Awesome!"

Fearing God, you will want to hear how He blesses others.

Psalms 66:16

The Fear of The LORD is clean, enduring forever: His judgments are righteous…

Being nice in our hearts when we do things…

…that means our hearts are pure inside…we treat others well…we keep ourselves clean before God…

...and be careful of the words we say and how we say them.

Psalms 19:9-14

...and say nice things when we do

...and say nice things when we do

...and say nice things when we do

...and say nice things when we do

We are about to go…

Remember…
God Loves You and wants You to Love Him more than anything or anyone else.

He sent Jesus to die for our sins.
When we accept what God has done for us…

...that is called being saved - able to live with God forever.

But...

...you must come through Jesus first.

Come...
Hear...
Live forever in love, peace and joy!

Follow the righteousness of God-just being and doing right through God.

He helps us to do that through His Holy Spirit.

The Holy Spirit makes us strong and teaches us…

THE FEAR OF THE LORD!

The End…

…of this book, but a beginning…to love God more than ever before…

Lightning Source UK Ltd.
Milton Keynes UK
UKRC010959090120
356647UK00001B/11